W9-AFU-250

The College Survival Instruction Book

By Steve Mott and Susan Lutz

CAREER PRESS
3 Tice Road—P.O. Box 687
Franklin Lakes, NJ 07417
1-800-CAREER-1
201-848-0310 (NJ and outside U.S.)
FAX: 201-848-1727

Copyright © 1996 by Steve Mott and Susan Lutz

THE COLLEGE SURVIVAL INSTRUCTION BOOK
Cover design by Dean Johnson Design, Inc.
Printed in the U.S.A. by Book-mart Press

To order this title, please call toll-free 1-800-CAREER-1 (NJ and Canada: 201-848-0310) to order using VISA or MasterCard, or for further information on books from Career Press.

Library of Congress Cataloging-in-Publication Data
Mott, Steve, 1961-
    The college survival instruction book / by Steve Mott and Susan Lutz.
        p.   cm.
    ISBN 1-56414-248-5 (paper)
    1. College student orientation–United States.   I. Lutz, Susan, 1964-   . II. Title.
LB2343.32.M68 1996
378.1'98–dc20

                                                                96-20939
                                                                CIP

To Lola and Blue

❧❧❧❧

Special thanks to Randy Cobb, Jackie Brown, Bill Bonekemper of Demand Printing, Joseph-Beth Booksellers, Jack York, David Lockard, Frank Lark, Laurie Rosen Marcus, Jeff Herman, and to the many others who offered ideas and support.

Contents

৵৵৵৵

Contents

Introduction

College is a special time in any person's life. Where else can you study philosophy in the morning, play mud football in the afternoon, attend a jazz recital in the evening and dance on the furniture at midnight? In terms of opportunities per square foot, a college campus just can't be beat.

College also represents a challenging transition. Going to college means a new address, new friends, new relationships with family members, new responsibilities, new knowledge and new freedom. It is a period of simultaneous confusion, excitement and growth.

This book provides suggestions and ideas for all areas of college life—academics, dorm life, extracurricular activi people, social life, the arts and family.

We've also included a "Getting started" section that foc on preparing for and moving to college. Be sure to read it and pass the information on to your future roommate well as your other college-bound friends.

We want to stress that this is an *idea* book. There are hundreds of great ideas here and we encourage you to those that interest you. But we could never capture all possibilities of a college career in any book. More than anything, we hope our ideas will help to inspire *your own* ideas for success and adventure on campus.

If you would like to share your ideas, we'd love to hear from you. Write us in care of the publisher, or e-mail us at steve@demand.com.

❧❧❧❧

Getting started

❧❧❧❧

As an incoming freshman, it is only natural to experience a mixture of excitement and apprehension. Moving from the comfort of your home to the vast unknown of a college campus may seem a bit intimidating, but it will prove to be a rewarding step forward. After even a few days on campus, you'll begin to feel that your new home is like—home. Because you are entering a whole new world, it is difficult to know what to bring with you. In general, we recommend underpacking rather than overpacking, but we've listed several necessities that you should not leave home without.

We encourage you to arrive on campus a few days before classes start, if possible. Attend as many of the orientation events as possible, while also taking plenty of time to simply wander around campus and get your bearings.

On the following pages are some tips for your preparation, arrival and first few days on campus.

Visit your campus before school starts, if possible, and find the library, the bookstore, your dorm, the registration office and the student center.

❧❧❧❧

On arrival day, offer to help people move into the dorm. You'll make instant friends.

❧❧❧❧

Invest in a good dictionary.

Contact your new roommate before school starts:

- •Call, write or e-mail him or her so you're not total strangers when you meet in person.
- •Coordinate your "stuff." You need only one phone, answering machine, TV, VCR, stereo, iron, microwave.

⋰⋰⋰⋰

Expect a small closet and pack accordingly.

Bring dorm-room essentials:

- Hammer, screwdrivers and pliers.
- A couple of plates, eating utensils, a drinking glass and coffee mug.
- A plastic bucket for toiletries and plastic sandals for the grungy shower.
- Two sets of sheets and towels.
- A bathrobe.

Definitely *don't* bring:

- •Your entire CD collection. (Label the ones you do bring with your name.)
- •Your entire collection of anything.
- •High school trophies and press clippings.
- •Heirlooms or valuables.

∽∾∽∾

Pack in soft-sided luggage that can be stored efficiently.

Photocopy everything in your wallet or purse (except cash and condoms) front and back. Keep one copy and leave one with your parents.

❦❦❦❦

Get a calling card for emergency calls from the road.

❦❦❦❦

Rent a mini-fridge, but never defrost it.

If you have a car on campus:

- •Get the necessary parking permits immediately.
- •Join a road service or auto club, such as AAA.

ఈఈఈఈ

Get on the mailing list for the ski club, arts society, film society, lecture series and anything else that interests you.

Before you need them:

- Learn the campus buses and/or shuttle services.
- Memorize the number for the campus police.
- Know where to go for injuries, toothaches, birth control and other medical needs.

∽∽∾∾

Forget your SAT scores, ACT scores and high school GPA. They don't matter anymore.

The art of college

There's so much to learn, see and experience on a college campus, that you'll only scratch the surface in four years. So it's important to get started immediately. Our best advice is to maintain a balance between academics and other activities, and to fully explore the diverse possibilities of life on campus. Here are lots of ideas for making the most of your college career. They range from practical to creative to whimsical. Campus life should be a combination of all three.

Let the adventure begin!

Consider registering for classes as an important right, not an unavoidable nuisance.

လၵ္သာ

Do not be intimidated by course offerings that read: "By Permission of Instructor Only." Find the professor and get permission to register.

ఆఆఅఅ

Check the finals schedule before registration. Make sure they're not bunched too tightly.

Take your hardest schedules in the fall and winter.

৵৵৵৵

Never take more than one "Intro to..." class at a time.

৵৵৵৵

Find the cheapest and fastest place to make copies.
You'll visit it often.

Be a money manager:

- Take advantage of student discounts.

- Don't waste money on parking. Walk or bike as much as possible.

- Record every transaction in your checkbook, especially ATM withdrawals.

- Establish good credit by opening a VISA account and keeping your balance under control.

Carry mace. Know which routes are lit at night. Travel in pairs. Think safe.

৵৵৵৵

Be green. Find out how to recycle and make it a habit.

৵৵৵৵

Keep a journal.

Rush, even if you're not sold on Greek life. It's a great way to meet people.

ক্ষ-ক্ষ-ক্ষ-ক্ষ

Get through a crisis on your own. You'll be surprised what you can achieve. The experience will teach you to tap into your own resources, learn your own power, and not rely on Mom and Dad, teachers or resident assistants to "hold your hand."

Use e-mail to correspond with family and friends. Because it's easy, immediate and doesn't require envelopes or stamps, you're less likely to procrastinate.

Don't blow financial aid or anything else by missing filing deadlines.

Put some discipline in your life:

- Keep a planner/calendar in your bookbag and record all assignment due dates immediately.
- Set your alarm to the buzzer, not the radio.
- Don't let your clothes sit in the laundry room. They may get dirty, wrinkled or even stolen if you leave them too long.
- Abstain from something you crave for an entire semester. Willpower is a great skill to develop.

Exercise your body, as well as your mind:
- Play mud football.
- Ride the bike trails.
- Sweat the fitness trail.
- Take yoga or karate classes.

Master the library as soon as possible.

Go to a museum every semester, even if it's not related to a class you're taking.

જ્જ્જ્જ

If you have a long drive home for the holidays, find a rider on the ride board to help defray expenses—and make new acquaintances.

Earn pizza money by being a subject in psychology experiments. Check psych department bulletin boards for notices.

ৰ্জ-ৰ্জ-ৰ্জ-ৰ্জ

Pay parking tickets promptly, but get your revenge— use pennies.

ৰ্জ-ৰ্জ-ৰ্জ-ৰ্জ

Vote. Request absentee ballots early.

See classic films, and films that *should* be classics:

- *Citizen Kane.*
- Any film by that Akiro guy.
- *A Clockwork Orange.*
- *The Delicatessen*—a particularly dark French comedy.
- *Short Cuts*.
- Every Woody Allen movie. Or none of them.

Be the first person you know to line up a summer job. Christmas break is not too early to start hunting.

߷߷߷߷

Wear your bathrobe on the way to the shower. You're not on *NYPD Blue*.

߷߷߷߷

If you're sexually active, have an AIDS test, use condoms and be honest with your partner.

Entertain with flair:

- •Have a retro party. Play LP records on a turntable.

- •Host a slumber party.

- •Organize a pig roast.

Resist the temptation to hassle the campus security cops.

Open a checking account at school; you'll save ATM charges and avoid the hassle of cashing out-of-state checks.

৵৵৵৵

Avoid the ATM. It is your enemy.

৵৵৵৵

Smoke a cigar. Then quit smoking forever.

Live at least one year in an off-campus apartment. It provides a different perspective and real-life experience with such skills as rent paying, utilities budgeting and landlord relations.

Rebel against the skill you developed so fully in high school—making excuses.

Subscribe to at least one magazine each year. May we suggest:

- Freshman: *Rolling Stone.*
- Sophomore: *Interview.*
- Junior: *Spy.*
- Senior: *Atlantic Monthly.*

Refuse to haze or be hazed.

Treat yourself right:

- Allow yourself one sleep-in morning a week, but not seven.

- Reward yourself for a job well-done. Choose a new CD, see a movie, eat a hot fudge sundae.

- Wear your jammies to the cafeteria.

- Invite yourself to someone's apartment to cook yourself a decent meal.

Pick up at least one of these habits: *The Wall Street Journal, The New Yorker*, National Public Radio.

෯෯෯෯

Convert a skill into spending money:

- •Start a word processing business.
- •Sew curtains and sell them to fellow students.
- •Start a bike repair service.
- •Open a fast, cheap room cleaning service.

Attend every kind of religious ceremony you can find.

৵৵৵৵

Attend every ethnic festival you can find.

৵৵৵৵

Read *Heart of Darkness* and see *Apocalypse Now* on the same weekend.

Get out of your room!

ઌৡঌৡ

Let your creativity flow:

- Make a film. Have a gala first-showing party.
- Start a band. If no one will pay you to play, donate your services to a dorm party.
- Create a comic strip and submit it to the campus paper.
- Conduct campus tours and make up stuff.

Make a marked change to your appearance, at least temporarily. Shave your head, dye your hair, grow a beard, pierce something, get a tattoo. Or dare someone else to do so.

෨෨෨෨

Get a work study job, or any job you can find. Work off-campus if possible.

෨෨෨෨

Use a desk lamp. Most dorms are naturally dim.

Set a standard time to meet your friends in the library lounge for a study break.

Stay on campus at least one summer for classes or a summer job. The campus will have an entirely different and appealing pace in the summer.

Volunteer to work at a nursing home in town.

If the existing fraternities or sororities aren't right for you, start your own with your friends. Many national fraternities and sororities are seeking new colonies.

ക്ക്ക്ക

Be a winner—enter a talent, writing or engineering contest.

ക്ക്ക്ക

Learn as much as you can about the Internet and World Wide Web.

Study smart:

- Find an extremely private place to study.
- Learn to highlight—one sentence per page, max.
- Seek out a study partner for your toughest class.
- Study for finals off campus, if possible.
- Ask someone on a study date.

Protect your PC with an anti-virus program and surge suppressor.

჻჻჻჻

If your schedule allows, set a regular time to phone your family each week.

჻჻჻჻

Meet new people by volunteering to work at an all-campus event.

Attend MTV's Spring Break and find some way to get on the air.

Store nonvaluables at a friend's apartment over the summer instead of shipping it all back home.

Vacuum your floor...at least once a semester.

Be a late-night connoisseur:

- •Order pizza way too often.

- •Find an alternative to pizza that delivers. Try Chinese and Thai for starters.

- •"Acquire" condiments for emergency use.

෴෴෴෴

Never borrow a car without putting gas in it—more than you used.

There's nothing worse than being sick at school. Be sure to:

- Get your flu shot.
- Take vitamins.
- Wear a hat.

Go an entire day without saying "That sucks" or "That's cool."

Take a course in meteorology, "weather" you need it or not.

৵৵৵৵

Set a challenging goal at the beginning of each semester and make it happen:

•3.0 GPA.

•Perfect attendance.

•Two dates.

If you find yourself dreading school, do something about it. See a counselor, change your major, take a semester off, transfer. Don't spend four years and a million bucks in a funk.

෴෴

Trade sweatshirts with friends at other colleges.

෴෴

Date someone based solely on personality.

Find friends in the classroom:

- Share cookies or other treats with everyone in one of your classes.
- Let someone take advantage of you for notes, but only once.
- Get to know a professor. Maintain the relationship after the course ends.

Introduce yourself to someone who does not look like you, talk like you, worship like you or trace ancestry to the same continent.

&ßßßß

Be nice to the folks at the following offices: Registration, Financial Aid, Academic Affairs, the Bursar. You may need their help someday.

Be a good dorm neighbor:

- Be nice to your resident assistant. The job's tougher than it looks.

- Binge on care packages from home until you feel sick, then share them with your friends.

- Return the stuff you borrow before the owner has to ask.

- Pay your pizza debts. Nobody like a mooch.

Befriend the older man or woman who has returned
to college after all those years of working and/or
raising kids.

Know more than the next guy:
- •Learn the meaning of Post-Modernism.
- •Understand supply and demand.
- •Know Aristotle from Plato and Kafka from
  Kierkegaard.

Work at your campus radio station.

৵৵৵৵

Learn to drink coffee, and how to live without it.

৵৵৵৵

Listen to classical music: Elvis Presley, Van Morrison, Elvis Costello, Ray Charles.

Make your room a social center; keep your door open when you want visitors.

ക്ക്ക്

Appreciate the arts:

- •Know Monet from Manet. And Manet from David Mamet.
- •Know Stevie Ray Vaughan from Somerset Maugham.
- •Know Dada when you see it.

Develop a crush on a graduate assistant, but don't do anything about it.

❧❧❧❧

Respect the privacy of your roommate. If you've walked in on a tearful conversation between boyfriend/girlfriend, walk out.

❧❧❧❧

Take compromising photos at a party. Someday someone you know will run for political office.

Be nice to the dorky alums who show up for Homecoming. You'll be one soon enough.

≫≪≫≪

Date and be dated:

- Ask out the person you keep staring at in class.
- Go on a blind date, even if he or she is described as having a "great personality."
- Be honest with your hometown sweetheart. Or dump him or her.

Cling to your "undeclared" major as long as you can. Declare one, then change it.

When a friend shares his or her mother's cookies with you, send your friend's mother a thank-you note. More cookies will follow.

Commit random acts of kindness upon your roommate:

- Attend a class for your roommate when he or she can't make it.

- Never play the same CD more than five times in a row.

- Pop for a pizza if he or she is cramming for an exam.

- Proofread your roommate's papers.

Read *Zen and the Art of Motorcycle Maintenance.*

ৰ্জ-ৰ্জ-ৰ্জ-ৰ্জ

Meet new people creatively:

- •Every time you're in a line of three or more people, talk to one of them.

- •Collect signatures for a petition.

- •Referee intramural sports games.

- •Set up a lemonade stand on the first nice day.

Cherish your family:

- •Write your parents a letter and thank them for something important.

- •Invite younger siblings to visit you at school. Treat them well when they come.

- •Never brag or complain about the financial status of your parents.

Utilize your campus placement center:

- •Create your resume.

- •Sign up for interviews.

- •Practice your interviewing skills in role-plays with counselors.

- •Research industries and companies.

Attend the ballet, art openings, interpretive dance and every other kind of event you've never seen before.

ഔഔഔ

Write a note to one of your high school teachers who pushed you to be a better student. Or go back and visit.

Be selective in your friendships:

- Befriend the pizza guy.
- Befriend your roommate's family.
- Befriend the campus dogs and cats and the nice old people who work on campus.
- Beware the rugby team.

Be strategic:

- Refuse to fail. D is infinitely better that F.
- Learn the deadlines for dropping a class or taking an incomplete, before you need to use them.
- Use pass/fail options to explore courses outside your major.
- When your schedule is light, audit a class or two.
- Sit in the front row at least once.
- Sit in the back row at least once.

Read a chapter of whatever bizarre book is lying on the table at the library when you arrive.

తితితితి

Study abroad, regardless of your major:

- Take a semester, summer or entire year.

- Arrange your arrival/departure to maximize time for exploration.

- Apply for these programs early.

Read for pleasure no matter how swamped you are:

- •Read Raymond Carver.
- •Read Anne Tyler.
- •Read Eudora Welty.

Don't beg for additional points when you have an A locked up.

When in doubt, go for partial credit.

Read something, anything by Chekhov or Dostoevski. But not when you're feeling depressed.

Make a conscious decision to not cheat, and have the discipline to follow your decision.

Experience the library for more than just study:

- Make friends with the librarians.
- Use the library's listening room to broaden your musical horizons.
- Set off the book alarm at least once.
- Take a nap on every level of the library.

Take a graduate level class—especially if you are considering graduate school.

જાજીએએ

If you're considering law school, med school or business school, visit one *before* you start filling out applications. Talk to students. Sit in on classes.

જાજીએએ

Speak a foreign language every chance you get. Asking for lasagna in the cafeteria doesn't count.

Double your viewing pleasure:

- See *Harold and Maude*.
- See *Sid and Nancy*.
- See *Melvin and Howard*.
- See *Thelma and Louise*.

Take any class that has *Lolita* by Vladimir Nabokov on the reading list.

Improve yourself:

- •Give up video games forever.
- •Stop dotting your i's with circles or hearts.
- •Learn to tie a bow tie.
- •Master every software program you can. Learn Mac and PC. Learn marketable skills like graphic design or multimedia.

Drop a class, but only if it bores you. Never drop a class just because it is difficult, takes too much of your time or meets too early in the day.

❧❧❧❧

Take an introductory computer science class, even if you're an English major.

❧❧❧❧

Think ahead. Sit in on classes you'll be taking in future semesters. Pick professors carefully.

Save all your class notes for at least four years after graduation. You never know where your life will lead you.

ๅๅๅๅ

Learn to write, even if you are headed for a technical profession. Take composition classes until you make B or better.

Be yourself:

- If you join a fraternity or sorority, refuse to conform to its stereotyped image.

- Don't make any long-term decisions based solely on the expectations of your parents.

- Don't take political correctness to the extreme.

Take up crosswords, but not in class.

Host a visiting high school senior. If he's cool, show him a great time. If he's obnoxious, tell him you wish you went somewhere else.

Read 10 books over summer break each year. Real books. Get ahead by reading the fall semester reading list during the summer.

Foster a platonic relationship.

Learn a bar trick—anything clever that can be done with quarters, dollar bills, straws, napkins, and so forth.

ର୍ଶ୍ଚ୍ଚ

Organize a daily primal scream during finals week. Convene each evening and release your tensions with your lungs.

Be a booster:

- Attend your sports teams' road games.
- Climb the goal posts at the last game of the season, win or lose.
- Tailgate before and after football games.
- Support your College Bowl team, debate team and other notable eggheads.

If there's any hint of grad school in your future, take GRE, LSAT, GMAT or other exams by the fall of senior year—before you forget how to study.

శుత్తుళు

Select a minor and pursue it. The greater the contrast to your major, the better.

శుత్తుళు

Develop a code with your roommate for those times when you need a bit of privacy.

Forget basket-weaving:

- Take a music appreciation class.
- Take a modern dance class.
- Take musical instrument or voice lessons.
- Take a class in drawing, painting or sculpture.

Never take more than $3 to quarter-beer night.

Mix business and academics:

- Offer to work as an assistant to a professor, even for free.

- Seek out co-op and other work-and-learn programs. These are priceless experiences.

- Consider a foreign language that will differentiate you in the job market—Russian, Spanish, Japanese, Korean.

Value your professors:

- •Visit your professors during office hours.

- •Give honest feedback on professor/course evaluations, good or bad.

- •When you're stuck for a term paper topic, meet with your professor. He or she will do half your work for you.

- •Read a book written by one of your professors. Textbooks don't count.

Regardless of your major, minor in variety:

- Take at least one class that requires speaking in front of the class. If this is a phobia, take two.

- Take a psychology class. Diagnose your friends.

- Take a women's studies class.

- Take a business class from someone who works in the "real world" and teaches part-time.

Be book smart:

- •Buy used books. Because most people highlight the wrong things, buy the cleanest copies you can find.

- •Get a card at the local community library. Borrow, don't buy, the books for your literature classes.

- •Sell or trade in the textbooks you never read. Keep the better ones.

Fortify your resume without getting a job:

- Get certified as an aerobics instructor, personal trainer or massage therapist.
- Create a new board game and present it to game manufacturers.
- Develop a new all-campus event and pitch it to possible sponsors.
- Participate in a stock market investment contest.
- Start a club and secure university funding.

Pursue a new hobby:

- *Real* photography and film development.
- Fencing.
- Darts.
- Fashion design.
- Bird watching.

જાજાજ

Learn to tap a keg.

Hit the road:

- Make a weekend road trip to another school.
- Travel at least 100 miles to see a concert. Do not go by car.
- Make a pilgrimage to the grave of a fallen hero: Elvis, Lou Gehrig, Susan B. Anthony, River Phoenix or the dead person of your choice.
- During the summer, visit your college pals in their hometowns—or home countries.

Shed your high school skin:

- Grow out of your "computer geek" or "band nerd" image.
- Punt that terrible name your parents gave you and rename yourself to your liking.

≈≈≈≈

Be a groupie of a campus band, but not for very long.

Enjoy the best entertainment bargain anywhere—
attend a movie matinee every Saturday.

Get ahead. Take heavier class loads during your
freshmen, sophomore and junior years, so you can
focus on job hunting (or golf) as a senior.

Don't pin or be pinned.

Make a pact with your roommate to keep your room locked when you're out.

৵৵৵৵

Campaign for the commencement speaker of your choice, but start two years ahead.

৵৵৵৵

Never miss a TGIF party.

Party smartly:

- Beware of any punch served from a giant trash can and stirred with an oar.

- Have a party partner keep an eye on you, and vice versa.

- Don't kiss him or her unless you're prepared to deal with him or her after the beer wears off.

Stay up all night writing a paper if you absolutely must.

❧❧❧❧

Stay up all night watching Bill Murray films just because you want to.

❧❧❧❧

Learn the value of a degree by working as a laborer in the summer.

Save philosophy classes for senior year when you're at your introspective best.

Impress your date:

- Know the history and architecture of your campus.

- Memorize a poem to quote at a quiet moment.

- Know the flowers and trees of your campus.

Set a world record and publicize the effort, such as the longest continuous air hockey game.

જાજાજાજ

Learn the ultimate academic lesson: Smart is sexy.

જાજાજાજ

Nominate your campus dog, cat, meter maid, cafeteria cook or housemother for homecoming queen. And campaign relentlessly.

Forget Daytona Beach. Make spring break an adventure to remember:

- Go scuba diving or surfing.
- Camp in the wilds, or prospect for gold.
- Charter a sailboat in the Florida Keys.
- Go skiing, or mountain biking, or white water rafting.

Work on your attendance:

- •Attend campus drama productions, comedy shows, etc. Someday someone you see will be famous.

- •Attend any women's athletic event. Better yet, take a date.

- •Attend a fiction or poetry reading.

- •Attend a fencing match, or water polo, or some other unsupported club sport.

Don't ruin college by looking for your life mate.
There's plenty of time for that later.

Have the proper props:

- Throw rice and all that junk at *The Rocky Horror Picture Show*.

- Buy an inexpensive or used tux (they'll never know) and wear it every chance you get.

Treat your parents right:

- •Invite them to Parents' Weekend every year, and make time for them when they come.
- •Fax them the exam you aced.
- •Shock them. Show up at home without warning—and without a bag of dirty laundry.
- •If you remember only one important day each year, let it be Mother's Day.

Cross-dress for a day and use the experience for a sociology paper.

Push yourself:

- Survive a dance marathon.
- Live for a week on $3, even if you have plenty of cash.
- Perform at any amateur night.

When you outgrow your computer, donate it to a school or charity.

❧❧❧❧

Take a wine-tasting course during your senior year (if you are of legal age).

❧❧❧❧

Compete with your roommate. See who can go the longest without using "like" as an adjective or adverb.

Visit every building on campus and figure out what goes on in each.

Apply for any honorary societies for which you qualify. They almost never meet and they look good on your record.

Learn ballroom dancing.

Take a byte:

- If you're not a computer whiz, befriend one.
- Save your work every five or 10 minutes. Back up any long-term projects on diskette.
- Use the spellchecker before you print.
- If you buy a computer, look for educational discounts and go for all the RAM you can afford.

Feed your ears:

- Hear fascinating people you've never heard of at the various departments' lecture series.

- Listen to "World Cafe" on public radio.

- Enjoy the obtuse music of Tom Waits.

- Listen to Rusted Root and the BoDeans.

- Travel any distance to see the Barenaked Ladies in concert.

Rent all the goodies from the student center—inline skates, bikes, video cameras, pool tables, whatever.

Develop a ritual for 21st birthdays and enforce it within your circle of friends:

- •A special birthday costume to wear all day.

- •An embarrassing public performance.

- •An ad in the campus newspaper.

Start a fan club for the third string catcher on the baseball team. Make a big fuss—posters, membership cards, T-shirts, chants. Change that person's life.

Work on a political campaign.

Make an impression in job interviews: Bring your own business card.

Enter a float in the homecoming parade, something so outrageous people will talk about it for years.

ক্ষ্যপ্ত্যপ্ত

Read the Sunday *New York Times* with a friend.

ক্ষ্যপ্ত্যপ্ত

Play any co-ed intramural sport.

Be playful:

- Play lots of foosball, but never spin the rods.
- Find a backgammon, chess or Scrabble partner and play regularly.
- Play ultimate Frisbee, but never play hackysack.
- Play quarters, thumper and all the other drinking games. Get them out of your system.

Speak your mind:

- Go ahead, raise your hand. Tell the professor what you think.

- Send a coherent letter to the president of the university regarding an area that needs improvement.

- Submit a guest editorial to a local radio station.

Circle 50 items in this book that you want to do before graduating. And try to actually *do* them.

Explore bulletin boards in the science departments. Volunteer for archaeological digs, surveys, nature studies or urban exploration. You might even get cheap passage to a faraway place.

Expand your skills:

- Learn one or more of the following: SCUBA, CPR, American Sign Language, country line dancing.

- Learn how to fix a car.

- Learn how to shoot pool.

- Learn how to keep score in bowling.

- Train for and run a marathon.

Volunteer to call alumni to ask for donations. When you talk to someone friendly, ask for a job.

Put some jazz into your life. Start with CDs by Charlie Parker, Eddie Jefferson and Horace Silver.

If you go through rush, use an alias at the worst house, and tell some bizarre tale about yourself.

Get competitive:

- •Foster a heated rivalry with another dorm or house.
- •Play broomball, a wonderful game involving ice, sneakers and brooms.
- •Run for student government.
- •Compete with your roommate to see who can get better grades for the semester.

Wait in line all night or longer for some event that doesn't merit it.

❦❦❦❦

Act in a drama production, or do sets, costumes or lights.

❦❦❦❦

Sell spring break trips for a travel company. Your trip is free.

Enjoy these supreme road trips:
- New Orleans Jazz Fest.
- Chicago Blues Fest.
- Halloween in Madison, Wisconsin.
- Oktoberfest in Cincinnati, Toronto or Munich.
- Any "bowl" game.
- The Final Four.

Lend your support:

- •Become a Big Brother or Big Sister.
- •Join the coaching staff of a local scholastic team.
- •Tutor, either on campus or at a local high school.
- •Volunteer for a cause you believe in.

Go back to high school and talk to seniors about your college.

❧❧❧❧

Create your own home page, where friends and family can find you online.

❧❧❧❧

If you're a commuter, spend the night with a friend on campus once in a while. Or have a friend come home with you.

Stand out from the crowd:

- •Make a spectacle of yourself at a basketball game.

- •Dream up the most absurd or offensive name possible for your intramural sports team.

- •Have an opinion and defend it relentlessly.

- •Be different. Be responsible.

Stay at school over Thanksgiving. Find a real oven and learn to make grandma's stuffing recipe.

❧❧❧❧

Learn a new sport—squash, badminton, racquetball, golf.

❧❧❧❧

Don't lose your friends; before graduation, collect the home addresses of your buddies and their parents.

Watch what you eat:

- Gain the inevitable freshman 15, but not an ounce more.

- Make at least one meaningful substitution in your diet—yogurt for ice cream, juice for cola, fish for beef—and stick with it.

- Eat the worm. (Okay, it's not healthy, but you'll be the life of the party.)

Visit the Art Institute of Chicago, the Museum of Modern Art in New York City, the Smithsonian in Washington, D.C. — or Dollywood.

❧ ❧ ❧ ❧

Don't be afraid to negotiate with professors; offer to write a paper instead of taking an exam if the subject interests you.

Capture your college experience for the amusement of future generations:

- Take pictures of your friends—at class, on campus, at parties.

- Create a photo album each year.

- Make a video tape—a day in your life.

- Buy the yearbook.

Prepare for life after college:

- •Collect letters of recommendation *before* you need them.

- •Start building your network of possible job contacts.

- •Try to land internships or summer jobs where you have the potential for more contacts.

- •Keep a running list of achievements, awards, jobs and activities to include on your resume.

Reduce the deficit; be prepared to repay your student loans on schedule.

ややや

See *The Graduate*. Watch and learn.

ややや

Graduate.

About the authors

Steve Mott is a graduate of Northwestern University and the Graduate School of Business at the University of Chicago, egghead schools where students worry too much about grades. He found the same to be true when he taught business classes at Miami University. He lives in Cincinnati.

Susan Lutz is a few thesis pages away from her second masters degree from the University of Cincinnati, a large school where few students take advantage of the vast resources available to them. She held several positions promoting arts awareness at UC and now works at the Cincinnati Children's Museum.